SCHIRMER'S LIBRARY
OF MUSICAL CLASSICS

Vol. 60

CARL CZERNY

Op. 718

Twenty-Four

Piano Studies for
the Left Hand

Revised and Fingered by

WM. SCHARFENBERG

G. SCHIRMER, *Inc.*

DISTRIBUTED BY

HAL•LEONARD®
CORPORATION

7777 W. BLUEMOUND RD. P.O. BOX 13819 MILWAUKEE, WI 53213

24 Studies
for
The Left Hand.

Revised and fingered by
Wm Scharfenberg.

CARL CZERNY, Op. 718, Book I.

No. 1.

Allegro moderato.

a) As the left hand, in all of these Studies, is the important part, great care should be taken when practising it.

b) An excellent exercise. — Scales in connection with broken triads.

c) The eighths must be especially marked.

16295

Allegro moderato.

№ 2.

p dolce.

a) In order to execute well the double notes, so that the tones are heard simultaneously, not one after the other; it is recommended that the fingers first touch the keys and then give quickly the down pressure.

b)

c) Grace notes reckoned with the time-value of the note.

d) Very light, from the wrist only.

16295

6

Allegro.

No 3.

a) The melody of the upper voice well marked. The broken chords of the accompaniment very light, but clear.

16295

Allegretto vivace.

№ 4.

p leggiermente dolce

a) The skips here and on the following page, slowly, at first, until they can be made with entire certainty.

Allegro.

№ 5.

16295

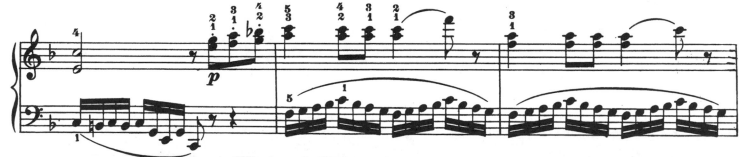

a) Between  C and C, no break.

16295

Allegro vivace.

№ 6.

Allegro moderato.

№ 7.

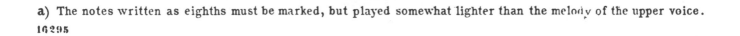

a) The notes written as eighths must be marked, but played somewhat lighter than the melody of the upper voice.

16295

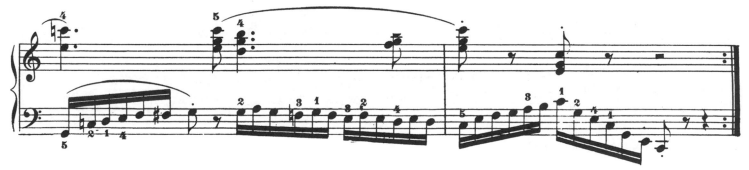

24 Studies
for
The Left Hand.

Revised and fingered by
Wm Scharfenberg.

C. CZERNY, Op. 718, Book II.

Moderato.

Nº 8.

a)

staccato.

cresc.

sempre staccato.

a) staccato, from the knuckle joint.

Copyright, 1892, by G. Schirmer.
Printed in the U. S. A.

Allegretto vivace.

No 9.

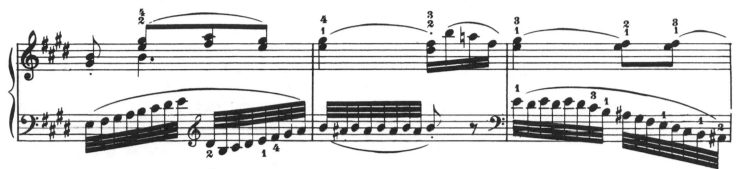

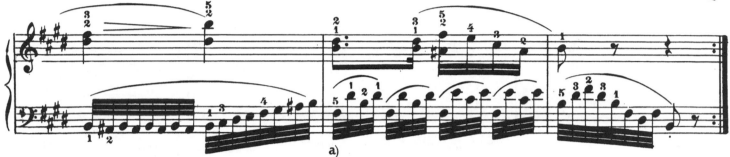

a)

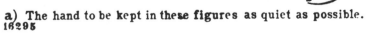

a)

a) The hand to be kept in these figures as quiet as possible.

16295

14

Allegro.

No 10.

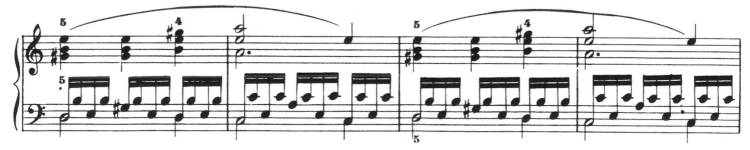

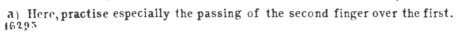
a) Here, practise especially the passing of the second finger over the first.

16295

Allegretto vivace.

N.º 11.

16295

Allegretto scherzoso.

Nº 12.

a) Preparatory study with strong touch
b) The double notes to be practiced as in Nº 2.

Allegretto.

№ 13.

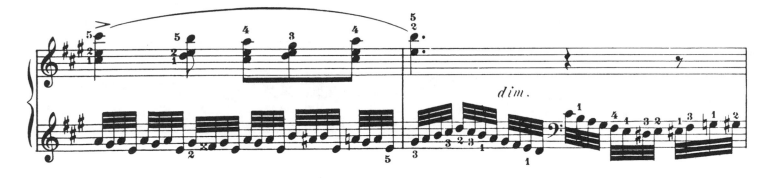

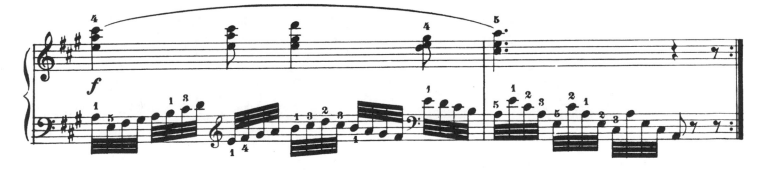

18

a) Execution of double grace-note, which would be written thus:

16295

№15.

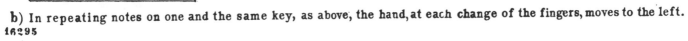

a)

b) In repeating notes on one and the same key, as above, the hand, at each change of the fingers, moves to the left.

16295

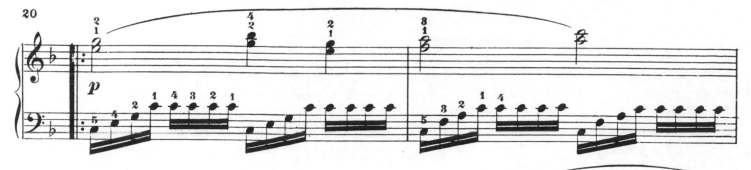

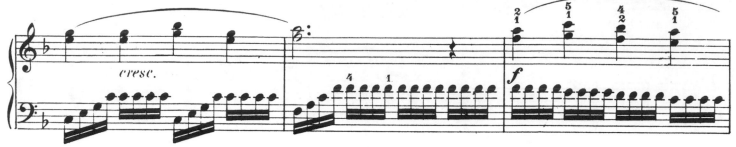

№ 10.

Allegro vivace.

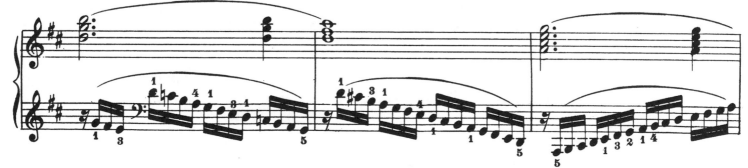

24 Studies
for
The Left Hand.

Revised and fingered by
Wm Schurfenberg.

C. CZERNY, Op.718. Book III.

Allegretto.

№ 17.

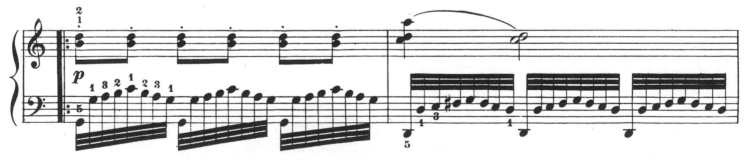

a) A very useful exercise to strengthen the 4th and 5th fingers.

13295

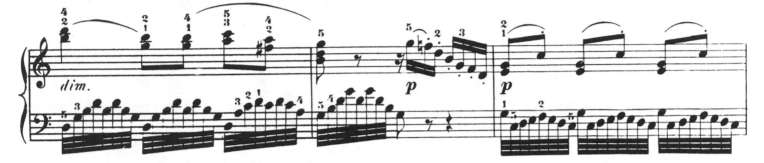

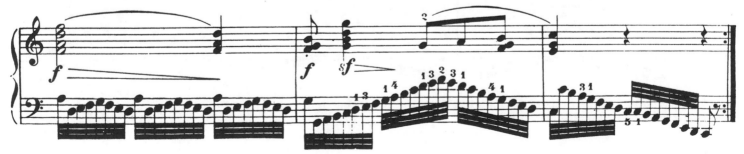

16295

Allegretto vivace.

N. 18.

a) The time value of the grace-note is taken from the preceding note, in order to mark the $f\sharp$ with the proper accent. The two small notes, therefore, are played with the sixth 16th of the measure.

Allegro vivace.

N⁰ 19.

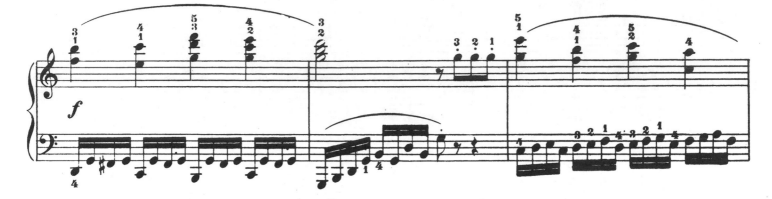

№ 20.

Allegretto.

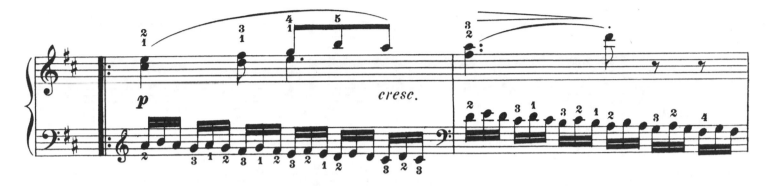

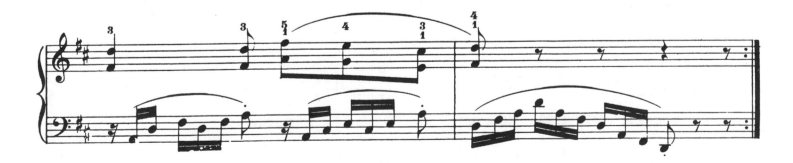

Allegro commodo.

N.º 21.

Allegro moderato.

N.º 22.

Moderato.

N⁰ 23.

a)   b)   c) End of trill on *B♭* thus:

N°24.

Allegro vivace.

16295

a) Do not play this too often in succession with the left hand, causing an overstraining of the wrist. As soon as the least weariness is felt, refrain from playing.